Fire Boats

by Marcia S. Freeman

Consulting Editor:
Gail Saunders-Smith, Ph.D.

Consultant:
Mark Edelbrock
Fire Boat Pilot
Seattle Fire Department

Pebble Books

an imprint of Capstone Press
Mankato, Minnesota

Pebble Books are published by Capstone Press
818 North Willow Street, Mankato, Minnesota 56001
http://www.capstone-press.com

Library of Congress Cataloging-in-Publication Data
Freeman, Marcia S. (Marcia Sheehan), 1937–
    Fire boats/by Marcia S. Freeman.
    p. cm.—(Community vehicles)
    Includes bibliographical references and index.
    Summary: Describes fire boats, the equipment they carry, and the work they do.
    ISBN 0-7368-0101-4
    1. Fireboats—Juvenile literature. [1. Fireboats.] I. Title. II. Series.
TH9391.F74 1999
623.8′65—dc21   98-4250
                                                                                       CIP
                                                                                       AC

Note to Parents and Teachers

This series supports national social studies standards related to authority and government. This book describes and illustrates fire boats and the equipment they carry. The photographs support early readers in understanding the text. The sentence structures offer subtle challenges. This book introduces early readers to vocabulary used in this subject area. The vocabulary is defined in the Words to Know section. Early readers may need assistance in reading some words and in using the Table of Contents, Words to Know, Read More, Internet Sites, and Index/Word List sections of the book.

Table of Contents

Fire Boats 5

Tools 7

Note to Parents and Teachers . . . 2

Words to Know 22

Read More 23

Internet Sites 23

Index/Word List 24

Fire boats work on the water. Fire fighters use fire boats to fight fires on boats and docks.

Fire boats have horns and flashing lights. Horns and lights tell people that fire boats are coming.

Fire boats have pilot houses. Fire fighters use controls in pilot houses to run fire boats. Fire boat pilots steer fire boats.

Fire boats have monitors.
Fire fighters use monitors
to spray water on fires.
Pumps draw water from
under the boat.

Fire boats have hoses. Fire fighters use hoses to spray water or foam on fires. Foam puts out fires that water cannot put out.

search lights

FIRE RESCUE

CHIEF SEATTLE

Fire boats have bright search lights. They light up the scene of a fire. Search lights help fire fighters find people in the water.

Some fire boats have dinghies. Fire fighters use these small boats to save people. Dinghies can go into places that large fire boats cannot reach.

Fire boats have ladders.
Divers can go down the
ladders to the water.
Divers save people who
are in the water.

Fire boats dock at fire stations after fires. Fire fighters keep fire boats ready to fight fires.

Words to Know

controls—levers and switches used to make something work

dinghy—a small boat with a motor

foam—many small bubbles; fire fighting foam is made from a special liquid.

horn—a machine that makes a loud sound

hose—a long, bendable tube that carries water or foam from one place to another

monitor—a pipe through which water or foam is sprayed; monitors on fire boats can spray a column of water 295 feet (90 meters).

pilot house—the room on a fire boat that has the boat's controls

pump—a machine that forces liquid from one place to another; fire boat pumps force water or foam to monitors.

Read More

Gibbons, Gail. *Emergency!* New York: Holiday House, 1994.

Ready, Dee. *Fire Fighters.* Community Helpers. Mankato, Minn.: Bridgestone Books, 1997.

Somerville, Louisa. *Rescue Vehicles.* Look Inside Cross-Sections. New York: Dorling Kindersley, 1995.

Internet Sites

Fire Safe Kids Page
http://www.state.il.us/kids/fire

USFA Kids Homepage
http://www.usfa.fema.gov/kids/index.htm

Index/Word List

boat, 5, 11, 17
controls, 9
dinghies, 17
divers, 19
docks, 5
fire, 5, 11, 13, 15, 21
fire fighters, 5, 9, 11, 13, 15, 17, 21
fire stations, 21
flashing lights, 7
foam, 13

horns, 7
hoses, 13
ladders, 19
monitors, 11
pilot houses, 9
pilots, 9
places, 17
pumps, 11
scene, 15
search lights, 15
water, 5, 11, 13, 15, 19

Word Count: 188
Early-Intervention Level: 10

Editorial Credits
Colleen Sexton, editor; Clay Schotzko/Icon Productions, cover designer;
    Sheri Gosewisch, photo researcher

Photo Credits
Dan Polin, 16
International Stock/Ron Frehm, 4
Mark C. Ide, 18
Mark Turner, 6, 8, 14
Michele Burgess, cover
Phillip Roullard, 12
PhotoBank, Inc./Mary Ann Hemphill, 10
Valan Photos/Arthur Burchell, 1; Ken Cole, 20